Dedicated

To my husband, children, family and close friends: Thank you for supporting me throughout the writing of this book.

CHAPTER 1
SCHOOL'S OUT

It was the last Friday of the summer term. Trevor, who was five years old and his three-year old brother Terence were so excited to be breaking up for the summer holidays and could not wait until the final bell went. Little did they know what Mum and Dad had planned for them.

Brrrrrg! Brrrrg! The final bell went. Trevor and Terence grabbed their bags and ran out to meet Mum.

Both boys shouted, "Mum, Mum, are we doing anything special for the summer?" Smiling, Mum replied, "Boys, I have a few surprises in store."

No matter how many times they asked, Mum would not say what the surprises were, other than that they would be meeting new friends.

Trevor was so excited that he ran off to tell all his friends. "We're going somewhere special with Mum tomorrow, and we're meeting new friends!"

Terence was so excited that he just wanted the night to come so he could wake up to tomorrow.

When Dad got home from work that evening, the boys excitedly told him that Mum was taking them on a trip, and Dad would oversee looking after the house.

Dad picked both boys up in his arms and said, "Wow, how exciting!"

CHAPTER 2
THE DAY HAS COME

The boys were so excited that they were both up at 6.30am. Luckily, Mum had stayed up all night, packing all the things into the car for the adventure ahead.

Trevor asked, "So, Mum, where are we going?"

Mum replied, "We're going to London to see Debo and her two kids. Mimi's a girl. She's aged six, and Nini's a two-year old boy. But first, we must go to your football lesson."

Trevor ran up the stairs to tell Dad and Terence.

After a shower and breakfast, Trevor and Terence got dressed for their football class at 10am.

At football, Trevor played so well that he won man of the match and was given a trophy for the week. He was so excited about the trip that he told his teachers that he was off to London for a day to see friends, but he would be sure to bring the trophy back next Saturday.

While Trevor and Terence weren't looking, Mum returned the trophy to the coach and said, "They won't be around for a few weeks."

CHAPTER 3
THE ADVENTURE BEGINS

The trip to London took about three hours, so Mum told the boys to take a short nap since they'd just finished exercising.

An hour and a half into the journey, Terence woke up needing to use the toilet.

Mum had to stop at a service station so that everyone could go to the toilet and eat some food. It was an hour later before the journey started again.

To keep the boys busy for the other half of the journey, they watched movies on their tablet, but from time to time, they kept asking Mum, "Are we there yet?"

How much longer do we have?"

It was almost 4pm by the time they finally got to London. They were so excited to meet their new friends.

The boys and Mimi and Nini spent the rest of the afternoon in the garden, jumping in and out of the paddling pool. Meanwhile, Mum and Debo had a chat since they hadn't seen each other for two years.

The next morning, the boys were so sad
they had to leave their friends,
not knowing what lay ahead.

But Mum had another
surprise waiting.

The boys thought they were heading home, but Mum drove to London Gatwick airport to park the car.

The boys had puzzled looks on their faces.

Trevor asked, "Mum, what're we doing here?" Terence said, "Mum wants us to see the aeroplanes."

However, Mum explained, "We're going to Amsterdam to see Lexi and her family for a week."

Both boys exclaimed, "Wao!" Trevor said, "This is the best holiday ever."

CHAPTER 4
AMSTERDAM HERE WE COME

The flight to Amsterdam only took two hours, and Lexi's husband, Amos was waiting at the airport to pick them up.

He drove for an hour to the house, where they got to see Lexi and her son Danie, aged eight. The first thing they did on arrival was to run to the back garden to jump on the trampoline with Danie.

The house in Amsterdam looked so
different from houses in England.
The ceiling was higher and the stairs
so steep, you had to walk gently,
so you didn't fall.

Every morning they had breakfast,
followed by sunbathing or jumping on the
trampoline. Meanwhile, Mum packed their
goodie bags, ready for the adventure
ahead. From day trips to the park to trips
to the city on the bus to watch movies,
each day was different - except for the
first day, when everyone stayed indoors
to rest from the long journey.

Every night, Trevor and Terence called Dad back home to tell him about the day and how much fun they were having, while also missing him.

The day before the week was over, Terence had to pay a visit to the dentist because while playing, he had bumped his mouth. One of his tooth had to be taken out so that his 'big boy teeth' wasn't affected. He was such a brave boy and got some money from the tooth fairy that night.

Trevor and Terence had so much fun and didn't want the holiday to be over.
It was the day to return. Everyone was sad except Mum because she had another surprise planned.

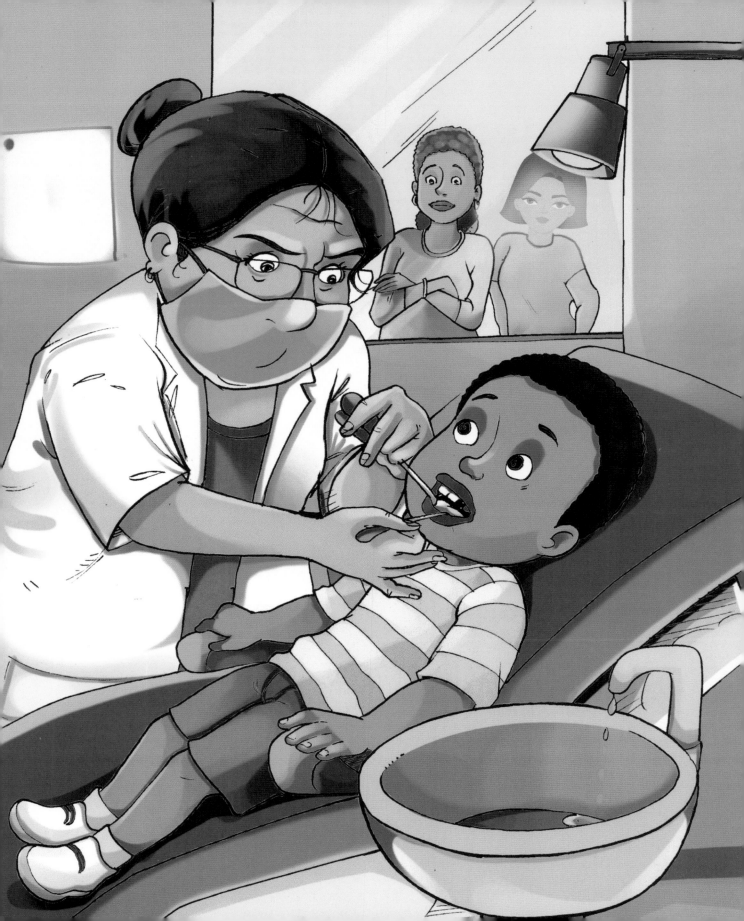

CHAPTER 5
ANOTHER ADVENTURE

Trevor and Terence were so sad that they didn't listen when Mum told the lady at the ticket counter where they were checking into.

Thank goodness
it was only a two-hour flight.

When they arrived, the boys
were confused.

Trevor said, "Mum, this place is different. Are we lost?"

Mum said, "No, we're not lost.
Welcome to Stockholm in Sweden."

The boys didn't know what to say.

Mum explained that they would be
staying here with her Great-Uncle Vee,
his wife Great-Auntie Ene and her two
grown-up children, Anie and Ite
for two weeks.

Great-Auntie Ene would take Trevor
and Terence to the park next to the house
for two hours every day. There were
slides, swings, climbing frames
and lots more.

Anie and Ite took three days off work to take Mum and the boys to various places. They went to the train museum, Skansen (an open-air museum), theme parks and even got on tour buses to explore the city.

On hot days when they weren't exploring the city, Mum and the boys would go down to the swimming pool opposite the house to cool down.

At the end of each day, Great-Auntie Ene always made a special Swedish meal for everyone.

Trevor even helped make pizza with Great-Auntie Ene, while Terence was painting with Great-Uncle Vee.

Trevor and Terence had an amazing time in Stockholm.

CHAPTER 6
THE FUN IS OVER

At the end of the two weeks, it was time to go home. Now, like Trevor and Terence, Mum was also sad as she had no more adventures planned.

They returned to London and Mum drove them back home from the airport, only stopping for a very short break on the way for them to eat and use the toilet.

When they got home, Trevor and Terence were so excited to see Dad, as they'd missed him so much. They both jumped on him at the same time. Little did they know, Dad also had a surprise waiting for them. It was chicken and chips from their favourite fast-food restaurant - yum!

Dad said, "How was the holiday?" Trevor and Terence replied, "It was the best time of our lives", and they had souvenirs to show Dad.

London

London is the capital of England and the United Kingdom. Here are three interesting facts about London.

- Big Ben: Big Ben is the world's most famous clock. It weighs 13.5 tons which is the size of two large African elephants, and it took 13 years to build.

- London Zoo: This was the first zoo in the world and is also the largest in the world. It was opened to everyone in 1847.

- People: There are over 8 million people in London, and they speak over 300 languages.

Amsterdam

Amsterdam is the capital of the Netherlands. Here are three interesting facts about Amsterdam.

• Amstelredamme: This is what Amsterdam was formerly known by. It was named after the river Amstel, where a dam was built in the 13th century to avoid floods.

• Bridges: There are more bridges in Amsterdam than in Venice (Italy). Amsterdam has 1,281 bridges while Venice has 409.

• Bicycles: There are more bicycles than people - with over 1 million bicycles and just over 860,000 people.

Stockholm

Stockholm is the capital of Sweden and is also the biggest city in Sweden. Here are three interesting facts about Stockholm.

• Museum: The world's first open-air museum can be found in Stockholm, and it's called Skansen (which means scones). It recreates Swedish life in different ages and has over 1.5 million visitors each year.

• Art Gallery: The world's longest art gallery can be found in the Odenplan metro station in Stockholm. It was opened in 2009, and there's a giant piano keyboard you can play by stepping on it!

• Islands: Stockholm sits on 14 islands and has 57 bridges and 96 beaches. It has the nickname 'Beauty on the Water'.

Printed in Great Britain
by Amazon

77223900R00027